Electrical Circuits and Currents

Barbara Somervill

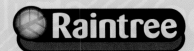

www.raintreepublishers.co.uk
Visit our website to find out more information about Raintree books.

To order:
☎ Phone 44 (0) 1865 888112
📄 Send a fax to 44 (0) 1865 314091
💻 Visit the Raintree Bookshop at www.raintreepublishers.co.uk to browse our catalogue and order online.

Raintree is an imprint of Pearson Education Limited, a company incorporated in England and Wales having its registered office at Edinburgh Gate, Harlow, Essex, CM20 2JE – Registered company number: 00872828

"Raintree" is a registered trademark of Pearson Education Limited.

Text © Pearson Education Limited 2009
First published in hardback in 2009
The moral rights of the proprietor have been asserted.

Edited by Megan Cotugno and Andrew Farrow
Designed by Philippa Jenkins
Original illustrations ©Pearson Education Ltd
Illustrated by KJA-artists.com
Picture research by Ruth Blair
Originated by Modern Age
Printed and bound in China by Leo Paper Group

ISBN 978 1 406210 68 2
13 12 11 10 09
10 9 8 7 6 5 4 3 2 1

British Library Cataloguing in Publication Data
A full catalogue record for this book is available from the British Library.

Acknowledgements
We would like to thank the following for allowing their pictures to be reproduced in this publication:
© Corbis/Gunter Marx Photography p. **32**; © Corbis/Michael A. Keller p. **24**; © Corbis/Miles/Zefa p. **33**; © Corbis/The Art Archive p. **21**; © Corbis/Walter Geiersperger p. **16**; © iStockphoto pp. **iii** (Contents, top), **34**; © iStockphoto/Brian Jackson p. **17**; © iStockphoto/Ermin Gutenberger p. **27**; © Photolibrary Group/Animals Animals p. **39**; © Photolibrary Group/Brand X Pictures p. **11**; © Photolibrary Group/photononstop p. **29**; © Science Photo Library/Adam Hart-Davis p. **5**; © Science Photo Library/Sheila Terry pp. **9, 12**; © Shutterstock background images and design features throughout; © Shutterstock/AM-Studio p. **30**; © Shutterstock/David Hyde p. **30**; © Shutterstock/design56 p. **37**

Cover photographs reproduced with permission of © Corbis/Douglas Keister **main**; © Corbis/Jim Sugar **inset**.

We would like to thank literacy consultant Nancy Harris and content consultant John Pucek for their invaluable assistance in the preparation of this book.

Every effort has been made to contact copyright holders of any material reproduced in this book. Any omissions will be rectified in subsequent printings if notice is given to the publishers.

Some words are shown in bold, like this. These words are explained in the glossary. You will find important information and definitions underlined, like this.

Contents

What do water and electricity have in common? Find out on page 34!

What does this symbol mean? Go to page 18 for the answer.

WHAT IS ELECTRICITY?

The alarm goes off at 6:30 a.m. You turn it off, and turn on the light. The clock, the light, and many other items in a home run on electricity. Humans make the electricity that set off your alarm clock. It comes into your home through wires. This is not the only place you come in contact with electricity. Electricity is everywhere. It is in the air you breathe. It makes your heart beat and your brain think. What is electricity?

Electricity = energy?

Electricity is a type of **energy**, like heat or wind. This energy occurs in **atoms**. Everything around us is made of atoms. Those atoms have tiny **particles** called **electrons**. The flow of electrons from one atom to another creates electricity.

Energy cannot be created or destroyed. It can only be converted from one form to another.

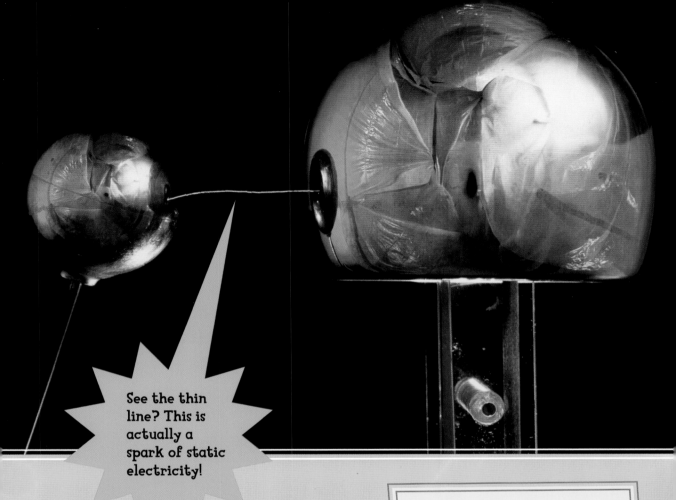

See the thin line? This is actually a spark of static electricity!

Electricity travels at 300,000 km/sec (186,000 miles/sec). If you travelled that fast, you could go around the world eight times in the time it takes to turn on a light switch.

In 1600 English doctor William Gilbert became the first person to use the term electricity. The word electricity comes from the Greek term "elecktra", or amber. For centuries, people made sparks of electricity by rubbing amber and wool together.

ELECTRICAL CHARGES

You step out of the car and onto the pavement. When you close the car door, you get a shock. How did this happen? You were the victim of an **electrical charge**. The charge built up in the car's metal frame and was discharged (released) when you touched the car door.

To understand what a charge is, you must enter the world of **atoms**. Tiny **particles** called **electrons** spend their time spinning around the centre of most atoms. These electrons move within the atom, and they can move to other atoms. <u>When the electrons move, the result is an electrical charge</u>.

Balance in atoms	Resulting charge
Equal **protons** and electrons	No charge
More electrons than protons	Negative charge (-)
More protons than electrons	Positive charge (+)

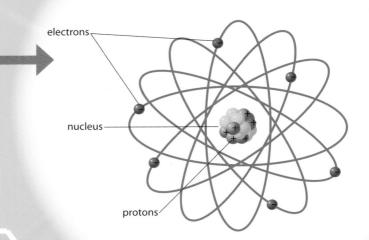

Six electrons circle around the nucleus of this atom. Look back at the table on page 6. What happens to the charge when there are more protons than electrons?

Science in action

Make your own **electroscope** to detect the presence of a charge.

Hypothesis: Metal strips in the presence of an electrical charge will follow the law of electrical charges. The strips will be attracted to a charged item if their charges are not the same. The strips will be repelled by an item if the charges are alike.

Materials: Aluminium foil, a glass jar, a paper clip, a piece of cardboard larger than the jar mouth, a strip of wool fabric, a metal ruler

What to do:

• Cut two narrow strips of aluminium foil, about 1 cm by 5 cm (0.4 in x 2 in).

• Bend the paper clip into a hook, inserting one end through the cardboard and the other through the two aluminium foil strips. Place the cardboard over the mouth of the jar so the aluminium foil strips hang down.

• Rub the wool rapidly over a metal ruler. Hold the wool next to the jar. What happens? Hold the ruler next to the jar. You have detected an electrical charge.

The law of electrical charges

The law of electrical charges is that like charges repel, and unlike charges attract. For example, two metal strips with negative charges will be forced away from each other. Two metal strips with opposite charges will be drawn to each other.

When lightning strikes

Storm clouds gather in the sky. What is happening inside these clouds? Drops of water and air are moving in the clouds, rubbing together, and creating an electrical charge. The faster the water and air move, the greater the charge that builds up. When the charge becomes too great, an **electrical discharge** occurs. We call this electrical discharge lightning.

LIGHTNING SAFETY!

Lightningisverydangerousforhumans.Lightningtakesthepath ofleastresistancetotheground.Ifahumanbeingisintheway,the lightningwilltravelthroughthatperson.Don'ttakechanceswith lightning. Stay safe by following these guidelines:

- Stay indoors. Do not talk on the phone, play video games, or take a bath. Lightning can travel along wires or pipes into your home.

- If you are outside, find shelter. A building is best, but acarwilldo.Ifyoutakeshelterinacar,donottouchanything metal on the car.

- If you cannot find shelter, do not hide under a tree or near anything tall, such as a flagpole or power line. Do not go in or near rivers, streams, or swimming pools. If you are in an open field, lie down on the ground. Lightning usually hits the tallest thing around, and you do not want it to be you.

> **umbrella + lightning = disaster**

Yes, an umbrella can attract lightning. Anything that makes you taller in a thunder and lightning storm can be dangerous.

A lightning bolt carries about 300 million **volts** of electricity. Two million car **batteries** do not carry as much electric potential as a lightning bolt.

Benjamin Franklin believed that lightning was a form of electricity. He flew a kite in a storm in hopes of forcing the electricity in lightning to travel down the kite string to a key at the end. Franklin's experiment was dangerous, and he was lucky not to have been seriously injured or killed. As a result of his experiment, Franklin invented the lightning rod to protect houses from being struck and burned by lightning.

Franklin developed some of the words we use today when talking about electricity. As you read about electricity in this book, look for these Benjamin Franklin terms: battery, **conductor**, **charge**, **discharge**, negative, and electric shock.

Benjamin Franklin ran many experiments dealing with electricity.

STATIC ELECTRICITY

You pull a sweater from the dryer and discover a sock stuck to the sweater. The "glue" that holds the sock and sweater together is **static electricity**. You walk across a carpet and get a shock when you touch the light switch. The electric shock also comes from static electricity.

Something that is static is not moving. Static electricity occurs when an electric charge builds up in a substance and has nowhere to go. Static electricity builds up between the sweater and socks because the items rub together. The **electrons** flow as the laundry tumbles in the dryer.

Some items collect more electrons than others. When the dryer stops, the electrons are caught. They have no place to **discharge**. If you pull the items apart quickly, you may see a spark. That is the static electricity being released.

Shocking!

One powerful static electrical shock can seriously damage a computer. People who work on computers prevent shocks by wearing **grounding straps** on their wrists. The grounding strap consists of a wire that touches the person's body. This metal to skin contact provides a way to slowly release the static electricity to the earth.

What kind of electricity causes this hair-raising experience?

Science in action

Here's an experiment to create static electricity.

Materials: A large balloon and a clean head of hair!

What you do:

• Blow up a large balloon.

• Rub the balloon on your hair.

• Slowly pull the balloon away from the head. What happens?
  The rubbing action makes the electrons in hair move onto the balloon.
  The balloon builds up static electricity and pulls the hair towards
  the balloon. You can also try sticking the balloon to the wall.

St. Elmo's Fire

It is 1593. A storm is brewing on the horizon. Sailors watch lightning bolts rip through the sky and wait to hear the roll of thunder. Strong winds blow, rattling the sails against the mast. Without warning blue flames dance on the mast. Fire on a sailing vessel could be deadly. Normally, the sailors would be frightened, but this is no ordinary fire. It is **St. Elmo's fire** – static electricity in action.

The tiny flames on the ship are St. Elmo's Fire.

A ghostly flame

St. Elmo's fire was not a rare event. Rome's emperor Julius Caesar wrote about it in his diary, and the Portuguese explorer Ferdinand Magellan mentioned St. Elmo's fire. How does St. Elmo's fire happen? In a storm with high winds and plenty of lightning, static electricity builds up in the air. The **charge** needs a place to discharge, and that discharge is a blue or blue-white glow.

The great sailing vessels of the 16th and 17th century are gone, but St. Elmo's fire is not. It is sometimes seen on the wing tips or tails of aeroplanes. For pilots, it is an excellent warning that a lightning strike might happen. Sometimes, the static electricity can also be heard as a hissing sound on the plane's radio.

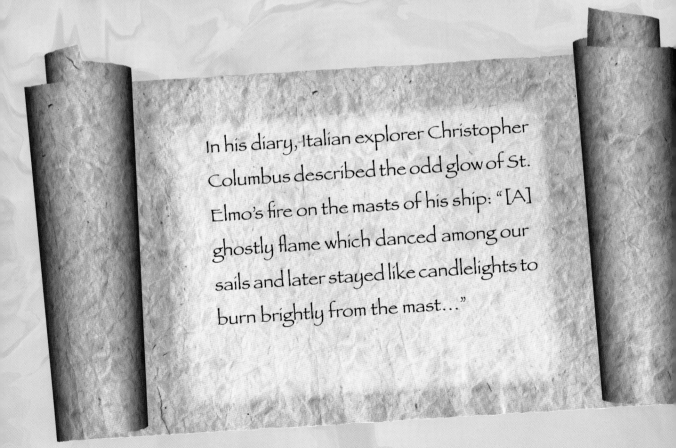

In his diary, Italian explorer Christopher Columbus described the odd glow of St. Elmo's fire on the masts of his ship: "[A] ghostly flame which danced among our sails and later stayed like candlelights to burn brightly from the mast…"

CREATING AND USING ELECTRICITY

Lightning strikes the earth thousands of times every day. Static electricity darts through the air around us. Together, they provide plenty of electricity, but the electricity is not in a useful form. It cannot be collected, distributed, or controlled.

To create electricity that we can control, we need to **generate** that electricity ourselves. Most electricity is generated using coal, oil, natural gas, nuclear power, or the power of flowing water, called **hydropower**. Electrical **energy** can also be generated by wind or solar power. We generate electrical energy in **power plants**. The most popular way plants produce electric power is by using a steam **turbine**.

Generating electricity

Here is one way to generate electricity: Fuel heats water in a boiler. As the water boils, it produces steam. Under great pressure, steam forces the turbine's blades to turn. As they turn, the blades spin a shaft connected to a generator. Inside the generator is a coiled copper wire. The shaft spins the coiled copper inside walls covered with **magnets**. The magnets force the **electrons** in the copper to flow from **atom** to atom. This action creates electricity. Strong magnets and many copper coils produce the greatest amount of electricity.

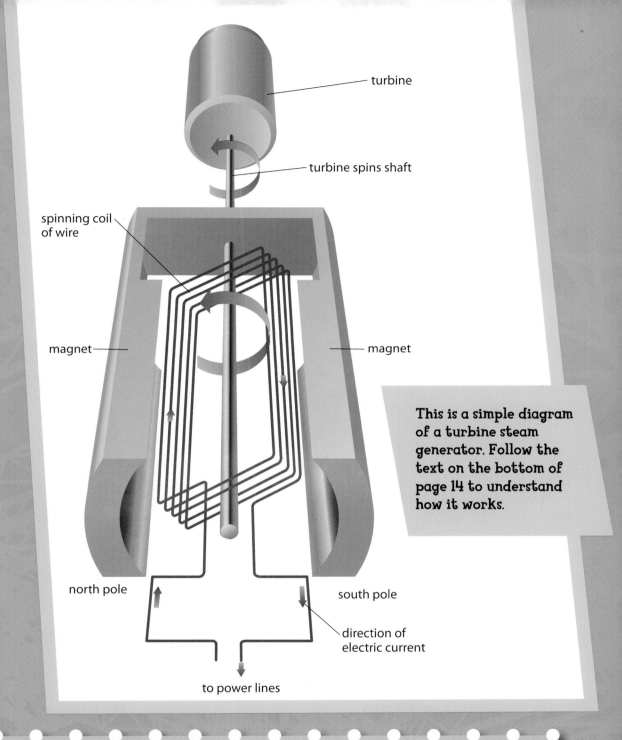

turbine

turbine spins shaft

spinning coil
of wire

magnet

magnet

This is a simple diagram
of a turbine steam
generator. Follow the
text on the bottom of
page 14 to understand
how it works.

north pole

south pole

direction of
electric current

to power lines

The world's biggest steam generators are in Neurath, Germany. This coal-burning power plant produces 2,100 megawatts of electricity. That is enough electricity to serve 800,000 homes.

Using electricity

Power plants use many sources to generate electricity. Some plants use fossil fuels to make power. Others use wind, the sun, or even rotting plants, called **biomass**. Once electricity is generated, it is distributed along power lines. The lines feed power to businesses, schools, homes – anywhere electricity is used. People also use portable electricity. That electricity is generated in **batteries** or power cells.

Power lines distribute electricity to homes, businesses, and schools.

The dashboard lights of a car glow with the power of electricity.

Loads

The items that use electricity are called **loads**. <u>A load is the power drained by any machine or electrical **circuit**.</u> The load may change electrical energy into another type of energy. For example, the load may change electricity into heat, light, or mechanical energy. A light bulb changes electrical energy into light. An electric guitar changes electrical energy into mechanical energy in the form of sound. An electric radiator changes electrical energy into heat. The amount of energy used in each instance is a load. <u>The more electricity used by a machine, the greater the load.</u>

Let's look at some of the loads on a car. These are parts of the car that run on electricity. Most cars run on petrol, but they also have an electrical system. That electrical system supplies power for many of the car's functions. When used in a car, the electrical energy may be changed into light, heat, or mechanical energy.

BASIC CIRCUITS

You push a button, and the television comes on. You flip a **switch**, and light appears at the end of a torch. You turn a knob, and a burner on the electric hob heats up. Those actions have each completed an electrical **circuit**. They opened a circuit to allow electricity to flow.

A circuit is simply a closed loop through which electrical charges can move continuously. A simple circuit has four parts: a power source, two connecting wires, and a **load**. You can make a complete circuit by connecting a **battery** (the power source) to a light bulb (the load) with a piece of wire. You also connect the other piece of wire from the light bulb to the other end of the battery.

You use these symbols when drawing circuit (schematic) diagrams.

Single cell

Battery

Connecting wire

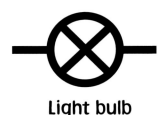

Light bulb

Switch (open)

Switch (closed)

Schematic diagrams

Here is a drawing of a simple circuit. Three D-cell batteries are wired together to provide power for the circuit. The batteries in this drawing are wired to three light bulbs. Electricians do not have time to neatly draw batteries or bulbs. Instead, they draw a schematic diagram of a circuit. They use symbols to represent the power source (battery), the pieces of wire, and the load (light bulbs).

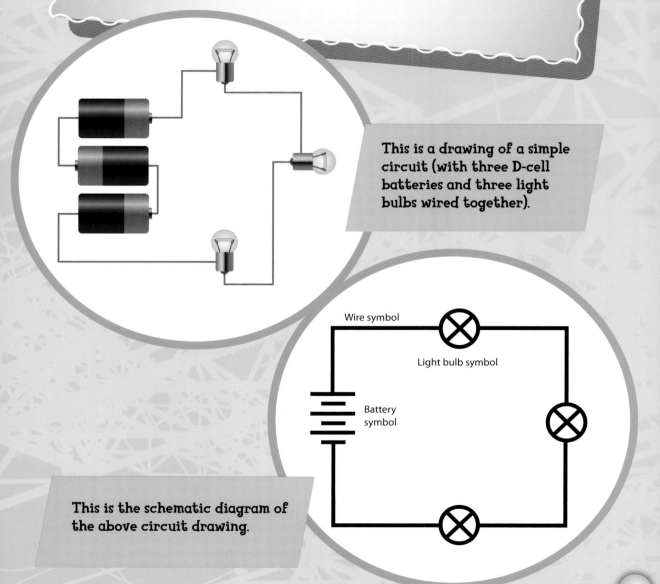

This is a drawing of a simple circuit (with three D-cell batteries and three light bulbs wired together).

Wire symbol

Light bulb symbol

Battery symbol

This is the schematic diagram of the above circuit drawing.

Wire it up!

You have a small light bulb, a battery, and some copper wire with bare ends. Draw a schematic diagram that represents how the three items will connect together so that the light bulb will light up.

First, look back at the symbols on page 18. Remember how to properly represent the wire, batteries, and load (light bulb). Then, look at the diagram on page 19. You will see that the battery must be attached to the wire at both ends to close the circuit. Start by looking at the pictures below. There are four different ways that the load can touch the battery. You can do the rest!

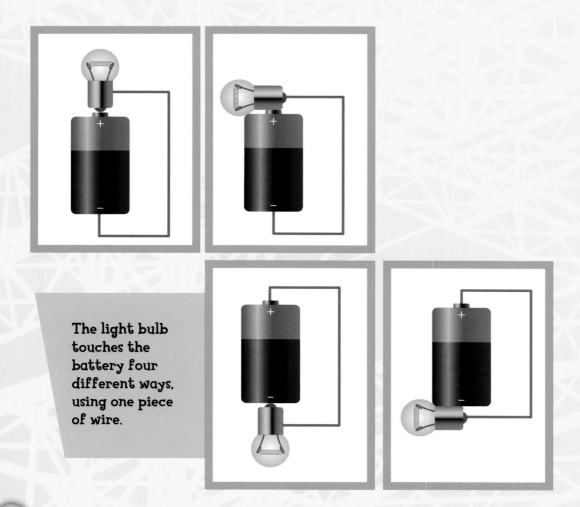

The light bulb touches the battery four different ways, using one piece of wire.

In 1800 Italian physicist Alessandro Volta developed the first battery, which he called a **voltaic cell**. In Volta's experiment, he used a pile of alternating disks of copper and zinc that he kept apart using cloth soaked in a salty liquid. He attached wires to each end of the pile of disks. Volta hung a frog's leg from a metal frame and attached one wire to the frame. When he touched the other wire to the frog's leg, it jumped! He had completed a circuit using a voltaic cell, or battery.

Series v. parallel

A shop has a burglar alarm to prevent robberies. A thief comes and breaks a window to get into the shop. Breaking the window also breaks the **circuit**, which triggers the alarm box. The alarm goes off, and the shop is safe. A burglar alarm is a circuit wired in series.

A **series circuit** has only one route for electricity to flow. There may be many **loads** and **switches** along the circuit, but the circuit itself is all in one continuous line. If the circuit is broken at any point, none of the loads will work.

At home, you turn off the kitchen light, but the refrigerator does not turn off. Appliances can be turned on and off and not affect each other. The appliances in a kitchen are wired in parallel.

A **parallel circuit** is wired differently. Parallel circuits have more than one route for electricity to flow. In this circuit, loads are wired side-by-side. If the circuit to any one load is broken, the rest continue to work.

series circuit

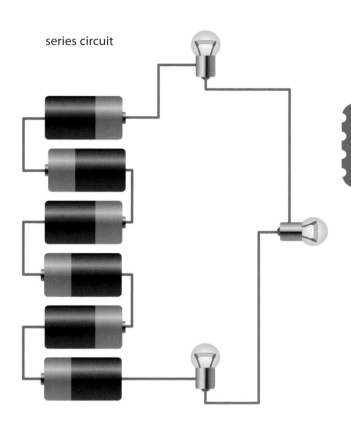

parallel circuit

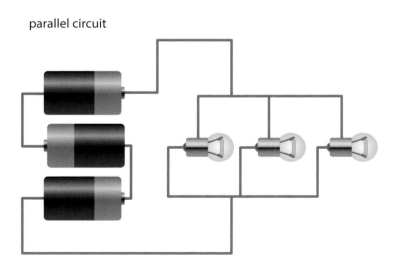

Science in action

You are planning the wiring for your bedroom. You will need to connect a lamp, a clock, and a CD player to the power source in your room. Draw the circuit diagram for your room using a parallel circuit.

CONDUCTORS

You plug your hairdryer into an electrical socket. You flip the **switch**, and the electricity flows. The materials that allow the electricity to flow are the metal prongs of the plug and the metal wire connecting the power source to the hairdryer.

An electrical **conductor** is a substance that allows the easy flow of electricity. Metals are generally good conductors. Some gases, such as neon, can conduct electricity. Liquids, such as mercury and salt water, also make good conductors.

Substances that prevent the flow of electricity are called **insulators.** The plastic covering on an electrical switch and the rubber coating around wire are examples of insulators. Without insulators, you would get a shock every time you turned on an electric appliance.

This plug is coated in rubber. The rubber acts as an insulator.

Why is the human body a good electrical conductor?

The human body is like a large sack of salt water. Inside your skin are many chemical compounds that are good electrical conductors: salt water, copper, carbon, zinc, and iron. This is why it is never a good idea to play around with electricity. Electricity can flow through your body as easily as it does through a copper wire. It can affect your nervous system, burn your skin or organs, and even damage your brain.

DO NOT PLAY AROUND WITH ELECTRICITY!

CONDUCTORS	INSULATORS
Silver, copper, gold, aluminium, iron, steel, brass, bronze, mercury, graphite, salt water, concrete	Glass, rubber, plastic, oil, asphalt, fibreglass, porcelain, quartz, dry cotton, dry paper, dry wood

Science in action: conductors in the home

Run an experiment that tests common household objects to see if they conduct electricity.

Hypothesis: Many, but not all, household items are good conductors of electricity.

MATERIALS:

• 1.5-**volt battery**, the type that is shaped like a box with **terminals** on top

• 3 pieces of insulated wire, about 10 cm (4 in) long, with the insulation removed from both ends

• a lamp socket with a light bulb

• household items: uncoated paper clip, coin, slice of lemon, slice of potato, pickle, bar of soap, crayon, fork, pencil lead, tea cup, nail, wooden spoon.

WHAT YOU DO:

Connect one wire to one terminal on the battery and one terminal on the lamp socket. Connect a second wire to the other terminal on the battery. Connect the third wire to the second terminal on the lamp socket. Screw in the light bulb. You should now have an open **circuit** with two wire ends that are not attached to anything. Those wire ends are your probes.

Place the uncoated metal paper clip on your work surface. Touch one wire probe to each end of the paper clip. Does the bulb light up? If so, a paper clip can conduct electricity. Test each household item in this way. Record your results, noting which items were conductors and which were not.

Were you surprised by any of the results?

SAFETY

It is fine to use a small battery for science experiments, but NEVER use the electric mains in your house. A small battery has very little power. It cannot hurt you. The electricity flowing through your house is dangerous and should be taken very seriously.

Ohms, volts, watts, and amps

The end of a light bulb is marked 60 W. A **battery** bears the label 9V. A **circuit** breaker is rated at 15 A. What do these letters – W, V, and A – mean? They stand for **watts, volts, and amperes** (amps). Each of these terms stands for a type of electrical measurement. Each term is named after a scientist who made discoveries in the world of electrical energy.

Think about electricity as if it were water in plumbing pipes. Sometimes, water comes out of pipes in a mere trickle. At other times, water comes out with great **force**. The amount of force pushing water through the pipes is called water pressure. The amount of force that pushes electricity through wires is called voltage.

Electric **current** is measured in amperes. It is the rate of flow of electricity through a current. In plumbing terms, it is the amount of water pouring through the pipes per second. **Resistance** is like the pipe size. Only a small amount of water can flow through a narrow pipe. This is also true for electricity. A single thin wire cannot carry as much electricity as a thick cable made up of many or thicker wires.

A light bulb that is labelled "60 W" would burn brighter than one labelled "15 W".

What is a watt?

A watt is a unit of electrical power. It was named after James Watt, who made many improvements on the design of the steam engine. The output of a **power plant** is measured in kilowatts, or units of thousands of watts.

A kilowatt-hour (kWh) is equal to the energy of 1,000 watts working for one hour. Electricity companies charge your family for each kilowatt-hour of electricity you use.

James Watt (1736-1819) was a Scottish mechanical engineer and inventor. His interests were not limited to electricity. During his lifetime, he invented many parts that improved the workings of steam engines. He also developed a device that could be added to a telescope and used for measuring distances. That device was helpful when he worked as a civil engineer and worked out canal routes.

What is a volt?

The term "volt" is named after Alessandro Volta. <u>A volt measures the force in an electrical circuit.</u> The higher the voltage is, the more energy that is released with every **charge** moving through the circuit. In the UK, a standard power line into your home delivers 230–240 volts. In the U.S., a standard power line into your home delivers 120 volts. If you plug an electric razor designed to work on 120 V into an outlet that delivers 230 V, the **motor** will burn up because the voltage is too high. (If you plug an electric razor designed to work on 230-240 V into an outlet that delivers 120 V, it will not work either.)

What is an ampere?

<u>An ampere tells how much electricity flows through wire that is one millimetre in diameter in one second.</u> Why do you need to know that? Suppose you want to plug a clothes dryer into a socket in the garage. Can the socket deliver sufficient current to run the dryer? Knowing the amperage needed can help you answer your question because some appliances need more current to run than others do. It takes more current to run a clothes dryer than it does to run a lamp or a radio.

What is an ohm?

An **ohm** measures electrical resistance. You can work out resistance using Ohm's law:

Ohm's law: I (current) = $\dfrac{\text{V (force or voltage)}}{\text{R (resistance)}}$

Explanation of Ohm's law: When trying to work out what the resistance, current, or voltage is in a circuit, use one of these formulas: $V = I \times R$, $R = V/I$, or $I = V/R$.

	is **ALWAYS** measured in	and is **WRITTEN** as
Current	AMPERES	I
Voltage	VOLTS	E or V
Resistance	OHMS	R

Georg Ohm (1787–1854) studied how different materials conducted electricity. Ohm worked out that the amount of current through a circuit is equal to the force of the electricity (voltage) divided by the resistance in the circuit.

Resistance

You are going through an obstacle course. You climb over a hedge and crawl through a tunnel. Every part of the obstacle course slows you down. This is what happens to electricity as it passes through wires and **loads**. It travels along an electrical version of an obstacle course.

Electricity travels through obstacles in a circuit board.

Circuits

Electricity travelling through wires and loads meets different types of **resistance**. Resistance slows down the flow of **charge**. **Electrons** moving through metal wire do not travel in a straight path. The wire is made up of **atoms**, and the atoms are obstacles on the electrons' path through the **circuit**. Wire, loads, and **switches** create resistance in an electrical circuit.

The device used in circuits to slow electrical flow is called a **resistor**. Resistors are probably the most commonly used electrical components. They are used to lower voltage and limit **current**. They can also act as heaters or **fuses**.

Work it out!

Electricity can be measured, just like any other fuel. With electricity, you measure the rate at which electricity produces work. Try working out this electrical problem. A 9-**volt battery** supplies power to a cordless curling iron with a resistance of 18 **ohms**. How much current is flowing through the curling iron? Use Ohm's law to find the answer. Check your answer at the bottom of the page.

The answer is 0.5 amperes.

Electrical currents

You press a button, and the microwave oven begins cooking a bag of popcorn. Although pressing the button and the oven's start seem to take place at the same time, they do not. Electricity begins to flow at the speed of light. The switch is on; a **circuit** is completed. Electric **current** begins to move. Water in a pipe or river flows in a certain direction. The flow of water is called the current. This is also true for electricity. When electricity flows, it moves. That is electric current.

Like the water in this river, electrical current also flows in one direction.

AC and DC

There are two types of electric current: **direct current**, called **DC**, and **alternating current**, called **AC**. Think of DC and AC like streets. DC is a one-way street; AC is a two-way street. Direct current moves in one direction. The electric current used to run a torch is DC. Alternating current flows first in one direction and then in the opposite direction. The current that runs your television or washing machine is AC. In fact, any device that runs off **batteries** uses DC. Any device that plugs into the wall uses AC.

Alternating current is a stream of **charges** that reverses direction. With AC current, this happens either 50 or 60 times every second. The rate at which the current changes is measured in cycles. Why do we have AC? It is cheaper to make large quantities of alternating current than it is to make an equal amount of direct current. That is because **power plants** can change the amount of power being delivered quickly and easily with AC. Over a long distance, DC power decreases. Over that same distance, AC power holds its charge. Power **switches**, power lines, and appliances that carry or use alternating current are cheaper to make.

Science in action

Do a power survey in your home. Make a list of 10 items that run on AC and 10 items that run on DC. Here's a start to your survey:

AC current	DC current
Bedside lamp	Battery-operated watch

Let there be light!

Flip the light switch. The light comes on. This simple action takes place in millions of homes every day. But exactly how does a light bulb change electricity into light? Light is another form of **energy** that can be released by an **atom**. Not all atoms can release light. However, most metal atoms glow when they heat up. The metal that glows in a light bulb is **tungsten**.

The inside of a light bulb has a glass mount, a tungsten coil, support wires, and inert gas.

The inert gas, such as argon, keeps oxygen from entering the bulb and burning out the tungsten coil. The gas does not react with other chemicals.

The actual bulb is a small glass balloon that fits into a metal base. When a switch is turned on, electricity travels through the metal base to the tungsten coil. The electricity makes the coil heat up. As it heats, the coil releases small atomic **particles** called photons. Releasing the photons creates light.

WOW! When electricity passes through tungsten, the metal heats up to a temperature of 2,200° C (4,000° F). This is about twice as hot as molten lava from a volcano.

The coil in a light bulb measures about 2.5 cm (1 in) long. However, the tungsten wire used to make the coil is actually 2 m (6.5 ft) long. It is tightly wound in the coil.

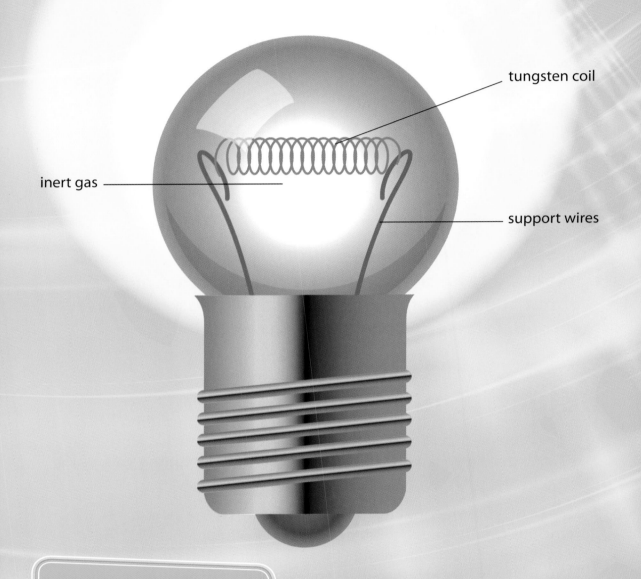

tungsten coil

inert gas

support wires

What actually glows in
a light bulb is tungsten,
which is a metal. As you
can see in this diagram, it is
wound in a tight coil.

Electricity in nature

Around the globe, 2,000 to 6,000 thunderstorms send lightning to Earth at any given moment. That means about 100 lightning bolts pierce the atmosphere every second. Ours is a very electric planet.

Electric eels

There is no place on Earth you can go to escape electricity. More than 500 fish that swim our oceans use it. **All animals, including you, use a form of electricity to control their bodies.**

One of the most fascinating electrical creatures is the electric eel. This ferocious creature zaps its prey with a shock of more than 600 **volts**. That is more electrical potential than what comes into your home! The eel uses lower electrical impulses to find their way through muddy water and find prey. Once the prey is found, the eel kicks up the voltage and shocks its prey. Eels also use their electrical impulses to communicate with other eels.

An eel delivers a powerful shock.

Electric fish

More than 2,000 years ago, the Roman doctor Galen used electric shocks from the torpedo fish to cure headaches and other health problems. The treatment must have helped the patients, because it was used by doctors from many other cultures.

Sharks on the hunt

Sharks can sense the electric impulses in other underwater animals. Saltwater is an excellent conductor of electricity, so sharks have no problem picking up these tiny jolts as they hunt.

39

The body electric

The body electric is your body. Every minute chemicals in your body combine to create electrical pulses. You touch a hot pan and burn your finger. The message from your finger to your brain is like email. It is an electric message carried along electronic paths – your **nerves**. You blink your eyes. You jump when you are frightened. All these actions happen because of electric pulses – tiny shocks that tell your nerves and muscles what to do.

One reason that an electric shock can kill you is because it disrupts your nervous system. Also, because the body is made of water, you can heat up or get burned. In fact, a very strong electrical charge can cook a human body. Electricity should be handled with great caution only by professionals.

In 1816 Mary Shelley wrote a great novel, *Frankenstein*. In the book, Dr Frankenstein builds a monster using various body parts. The doctor needs a massive jolt of electricity to bring the creature to life. Frankenstein gets that massive jolt from nature – from a bolt of lightning.

Frankenstein's monster came to life with a jolt of electricity!

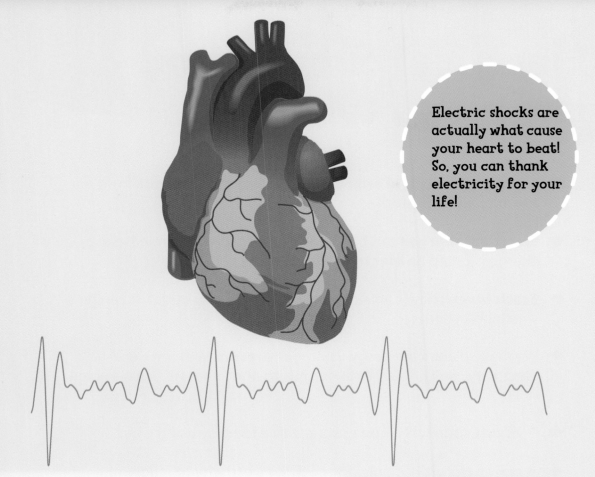

Electric shocks are actually what cause your heart to beat! So, you can thank electricity for your life!

A beating heart

Your heart beats because of millions of electrical shocks delivered throughout your life. What happens when your body does not send the correct messages to your heart? Doctors have developed an artificial way to deliver those regular shocks you need. A surgeon installs a **pacemaker** in a person's chest with a wire connecting to the heart. The pacemaker sends out regular pulses that keep the heart going…ka-thump…ka-thump…ka-thump.

WOW! If you could harness the power used by your brain, you could power a 10-watt light bulb. In fact, all your "thinking" is done by using electricity and chemicals.

41

Electrical circuits and currents review

◆ Electricity is a form of **energy**. It is the flow of **electrons** from one **atom** to another atom.

◆ **Electrical charges** can be positive or negative. The release of a charge is called an **electrical discharge**.

◆ **Static electricity** is an electrical charge with no outlet. It can be a shocking event!

◆ We make electrical energy using **generators**. When we use electricity, we change that energy into another form, such as heat or light.

◆ A **circuit** connects a power source to a **load** by using wire.

◆ A **series circuit** has only one path for electricity to follow. Parallel circuits wire loads side-by-side.

◆ A **conductor** allows electricity to flow easily.

◆ **Resistance** is a series of obstacles that slow the flow of electric **current**.

◆ **Ohm's** law states that current equals the **force** or **voltage** divided by resistance.

◆ Current is the flow of electricity. **DC** current flows in one direction; **AC** current flows in two directions.

◆ Electricity is found in part of every human body. We cannot live without it.

Quiz

1 Which of these substances would be a good conductor of electricity?

a. air
b. space
c. salt water
d. glass

2 What does an electrical circuit do in your home?

a. It protects your home against power cuts.
b. It prevents electricity from entering your home.
c. It makes a complete path that allows your family to use electrical appliances.
d. It protects family members from getting shocks.

3 Materials that allow electricity to flow easily through them are

a. conductors
b. insulators
c. generators
d. resistors

4 A device that opens and closes a circuit without disconnecting the wires is

a. a fuse
b. a battery
c. a switch
d. a light bulb

5 This measures resistance to the flow of electricity:

a. ohm
b. ampere
c. volt
d. farad

6 Which of these items provides power to a circuit?

a. a wire
b. a battery
c. a light bulb
b. a switch

7 When you get a shock from touching a doorknob, you are experiencing

a. direct current
b. static electricity
c. alternating current
d. a lightning strike

8 Which of these items does not conduct electricity?

a. a coin
b. a pickle
c. a tea cup
d. a paper clip

9 Which of these is the best place to be during a lightning storm?

a. in a bath
b. on an open golf course
c. under a tree
d. in a library

10 What is the unit used to measure the power used by a light bulb?

a. watts
b. volts
c. amperes
d. ohms

Electrical circuits and currents timeline

600 BCE	**Thales of Miletus describes what we now call static electricity, which he produced by rubbing metal with amber. This is the first reference to electricity written in history.**
1493 CE	**Christopher Columbus writes about St. Elmo's fire in his journal.**
1570	**William Gilbert (1540–1603) becomes the first to use the word electricity, from the Greek word for amber, elecktra.**
1729	**English scientist Stephen Gray (1696–1736) proves that electricity moves.**
1745	**Dutch scientist Pieter van Musschenbroek invents the "Leyden Jar", which stores static electricity.**
1752	**Benjamin Franklin runs his kite experiment and invents the lightning rod.**
1800	**Alessandro Volta invents the electric battery and proves that electricity can travel over wires.**
1826	**Georg Ohm develops Ohm's law.**
1888	**Charles Brush uses a windmill to produce electricity.**
1918	**Electric washing machines and refrigerators are invented.**
1953	**The first nuclear power station is built in Obninsk, Russia, to produce electricity by splitting atoms.**
2007	**Adelaide, Australia, begins using the world's first solar-powered, all-electric buses.**

Glossary

alternating current (AC) current that changes directions many times every second, like a two-way street

ampere unit of electric current used to measure the rate at which electricity flows through a substance

atom smallest particle of a chemical element that still has the properties of that element. Atoms are considered the "building blocks" of matter.

battery device that generates electric currents through the use of a chemical reaction; also stores electrical charges

biomass rotting plants that are used for fuel

charge group of electric particles collected together

circuit path along which electricity flows

conductor material that allows the easy flow of electricity

current flow of electrons, measured in amps

direct current (DC) current that flows in one direction all of the time, like a one-way street

discharge release of an electrical charge

electrical charge amount of electricity in something

electrical discharge sudden loss of excess charge from an object

electron one of the very small, negatively charged particles that are a part of atoms, found outside the atom's nucleus

electroscope early scientific instrument used to detect the presence of an electric charge on the body

energy measure of a system's ability to make things happen

force push or pull that gives energy to an object

fuse safety device; a piece of wire in a circuit that melts when the current is too large, breaking the circuit

generate to create electricity

generator machine that creates electricity

grounding strap device worn on the wrist to protect computers against electrostatic discharge. It is usually worn by computer technicians.

hydropower The power of flowing water

insulator any device that stops the flow of electricity

load power drained by any machine or electrical circuit

magnet object that can push or pull by using magnetic force

megawatt 1,000,000 watts or 1,000 kilowatts

motor machine that converts electrical energy into mechanical energy

nerve bundle of fibres that conduct electrical signals around the body

ohm unit that measures electrical resistance of a substance

pacemaker small battery placed under the skin with wires that lead to the heart. It measures heart rate and corrects a heartbeat that is too fast or too slow.

parallel circuit circuit that connects a power source, load, and conductors in multiple loops

particle tiny piece of matter

power plant place where huge generators are used to make electricity and send it to a community

proton positively charged particle found in every atom. Most electric currents are a flow of protons and electrons.

resistance material that discourages or slows the flow of electricity

resistor device used in circuits to slow electrical flow

series circuit circuit that connects a power source, load, and conductors in a single loop

static electricity electrical charge that builds up on an object due to friction

St. Elmo's fire electrical weather phenomenon; originates from a grounded object in an electric field

switch device for turning an electric current on or off, or for making or breaking a circuit

terminal point at which a circuit can be connected to a battery

tungsten metal that glows in a light bulb

turbine device that consists of a bladed wheel that is turned by the force of moving water, gas, or steam

volt unit of electrical force

voltaic cell first battery, created by Alessandro Volta

watt unit of power equal to volts times amps

Further information

Books

Blackout!: Electricity and Circuits, Anna Claybourne (Raintree, 2005)

Electricity, Steve Parker and Laura Buller (DK Eyewitness Books, 2005)

Electricity and Electrical Currents, Barbara Davis (Heinemann Library, 2007)

Science Files: Electricity and Magnetism, Chris Oxlade (Hodder Wayland, 2005)

Websites

www.eia.doe.gov/kids/energyfacts/sources/electricity.html
Learn more about electricity from the U.S. Department of Energy.

**http://www.bbc.co.uk/schools/ks3bitesize/science/physics/
electricity_intro.shtml**
This site provides clearly set out information to aid revision about electricity.

Scifiles.larc.nasa.gov/text/kids/D_Lab/acts_electric.html
On this site experts will help you to understand electricity.

www.edfenergy.com/powerup/keystage3/index.html
This site covers all aspects of electricity, including the effects on the human body and electrical safety at home.

www.hantsfire.gov.uk/electricity
Find out more about electricity as energy.

Look it up!

Do some more research on one or more of these topics:
• Nicola Tesla and AC
• Electric fish
• Pacemakers and the human heart
• Luigi Galvani and animal electricity

Disclaimer
All the Internet addresses (URLs) given in this book were valid at the time of going to press. However, due to the dynamic nature of the Internet, some addresses may have changed, or sites may have ceased to exist since publication. While the author and publishers regret any inconvenience this may cause readers, no responsibility for any such changes can be accepted by either the author or the publishers.

Index